W9-CJP-583

I Can Do It!
Kids with Physical Challenges

Kids with Special Needs

Seeing with Your Fingers:
Kids with Blindness and Visual Impairment

Listening with Your Eyes:
Kids Who Are Deaf and Hard of Hearing

My Name Is Not Slow:
Kids with Intellectual Disabilities

Sick All the Time: **Kids with Chronic Illness**

Something's Wrong!
Kids with Emotional Disturbance

Speed Racer: **Kids with Attention-Deficit/**
Hyperactivity Disorder

Finding My Voice: **Kids with Speech Impairment**

I Can Do It! **Kids with Physical Challenges**

The Hidden Child: **Kids with Autism**

What's Wrong with My Brain?
Kids with Brain Injury

Why Can't I Learn Like Everyone Else?
Kids with Learning Disabilities

I Can Do It!

Kids with Physical Challenges

by Sheila Stewart and Camden Flath

MASON CREST PUBLISHERS INC.
370 Reed Road
Broomall, Pennsylvania 19008
(866)MCP-BOOK (toll free)
www.masoncrest.com

First Printing
9 8 7 6 5 4 3 2 1

ISBN (set) 978-1-4222-1727-6   ISBN (pbk set) 978-1-4222-1918-8

Library of Congress Cataloging-in-Publication Data

Stewart, Sheila, 1975–
  I can do it! : kids with physical challenges / by Sheila Stewart and Camden Flath.
      p. cm.
  Includes bibliographical references and index.
  ISBN 978-1-4222-1723-8   ISBN (pbk) 978-1-4222-1926-3
  1. Children with disabilities—Juvenile literature. I. Flath, Camden, 1987– II.
Title.
  HV903.S755 2010
  362.4083—dc22
                        2010010010

Produced by Harding House Publishing Service, Inc.
www.hardinghousepages.com
Design by MK Bassett-Harvey.
Cover design by Torque Advertising Design.
Printed in the USA by Bang Printing.

Photo Credits
Creative Commons Attribution 2.0 Generic: DVIDSHUB: pg. 40, Honza Soukup: pg. 27; Creative Commons Attribution Share Alike 2.0 Generic: lunar caustic: pg. 29, tsuihin – TimoStudios: pg. 37, Daquella manera: pg. 39; GNU Free Documentation License, Version 1.2: Niteowlneils: pg. 39; LifeArt: pg. 33; United States Department of Defense: SSGT Harold Frasier: pg. 34.

The creators of this book have made every effort to provide accurate information, but it should not be used as a substitute for the help and services of trained professionals.

Introduction

To the Teacher

Kids with Special Needs provides a unique forum for demystifying a wide variety of childhood medical and developmental disabilities. Written to captivate an elementary-level audience, the books bring to life the challenges and triumphs experienced by children with common chronic conditions such as hearing loss, intellectual disability, physical differences, and speech difficulties. The topics are addressed frankly through a blend of fiction and fact.

This series is particularly important today as the number of children with special needs is on the rise. Over the last two decades, advances in pediatric medical techniques have allowed children who have chronic illnesses and disabilities to live longer, more functional lives. At the same time, IDEA, a federal law, guarantees their rights to equal educational opportunities. As a result, these children represent an increasingly visible part of North American population in all aspects of daily life. Students are exposed to peers with special needs in their classrooms, through extracurricular activities, and in the community. Often, young people have misperceptions and unanswered questions about a child's disabilities—and more important, his or her abilities. Many times, there is no vehicle for talking about these complex issues in a comfortable manner.

This series will encourage further conversation about these issues. Most important, the series promotes a greater comfort for its readers as they live, play, and study side by side with these children who have medical and developmental differences—kids with special needs.

—*Dr. Carolyn Bridgemohan*
Boston Pediatric Hospital/Harvard Medical School

"Hurry up, Sierra! You're going to be late!" Dad yelled down the hall.

"Coming!" I yelled back. I'm not usually late for school, but I'm always *almost* late. I grabbed my funky felt cloche hat and my video camera and wheeled out into the hall.

Dad was holding my backpack, which he hooked over the back of my wheelchair, and then he held the door so I could push myself outside.

Dad's car was waiting in the driveway. Papa, my other dad, had already left in the minivan to take

Lucy and Zoey, my four-year-old twin sisters, to pre-school.

I zoomed down the wheelchair ramp and turned as sharply as I could at the bottom. Dad hated it when I did that, but he didn't say anything. Once, I tried to see how fast I could go while I was filming, but because I was holding my video camera, I didn't have as much control and I tipped over. That kind of thing was why Dad didn't like me to zoom.

At the car, I pulled myself into the backseat, and Dad put my wheelchair in the trunk. My arms are pretty strong, but my legs are not, and I can't move my feet and ankles at all. I was born with spina bifida, which meant that part of my backbone didn't close up and some of my spinal cord poked out through the hole. They put it all back together right after I was born, but it messed up my legs for good. Most of the time, I don't mind much that I'm in a wheelchair. Dad and Papa adopted me when I was four months old, and they're good parents. When I watch Lucy and

Zoey running and jumping, though, sometimes I do get a little sad.

Dad dropped me off in front of the school, and I made it to class just before the bell rang. In the classroom, my desk was pretty close to the door. The reason for that was so I didn't have to steer my wheelchair around other desks, but it also made it easier to get in quickly and look like I hadn't almost been late.

"Hey, Sierra!" my friend Mia called, leaning over from two rows away. "My mom said she'll take us to the movies tomorrow if it's okay with your dads. Rachel might come too."

I started to answer her and say I'd ask, but then the bell rang and we had to stop talking.

Mostly, I paid attention during class. I'm usually a good student, and I do pretty well, but my mind did wander a few times. I started thinking about a movie I wanted to make. I made a movie last year that wasn't bad, kind of a modern version of *Snow White*. Of course, I was only nine when I made it, so there were things that I wished I could change when I watched it now.

Right before the end of the day, Mr. Nguyen told us he had an announcement. "We're going to be taking a field trip to Fort Symons next month, for our unit on the Revolutionary War." He held up a stack of paper. "I have some information here for your parents, and they'll need to sign a permission slip for you."

Everybody started talking at once, but then Michelle looked at me and said, "I guess you won't be going, will you? There are a lot of stairs at Fort Symons."

I wouldn't have even thought about the stairs at the fort if Michelle hadn't said something. Eventually, I would have, of course, since dealing with stairs was pretty much a fact of my life. But right then, when Mr. Nguyen was talking about the trip, I was thinking the same kinds of things as everyone else. Like, "Yippee! A field trip!" and "I wonder if we'll get the whole day off or have to go to a few classes."

"Of course, I'm going," I said to Michelle. "I don't care about the stairs."

"But what will you do?" she asked. "It won't be much fun to have to stay on the bus while everybody else explores the fort."

I glared at her. "Don't worry about it," I told her. "It's not your problem." Michelle never seems to like me, but this was worse than usual.

"But—" she started again, but I interrupted her.

"Hang on," I said, and pulled my video camera out of my backpack. "Whatever you're going to say, say it to the camera. I can use it in a documentary on how people feel about the disabled."

Michelle stared at me without saying anything, then narrowed her eyes and turned around. I felt a little better. Which was good, since for a second, I'd been afraid I was going cry.

I didn't cry about the thing with Michelle until we were eating supper that night. We were having fish and rice, and Lucy was complaining that she didn't like fish. Which made Zoey stop eating the fish, even though she usually liked it.

Papa tried to change the subject, so that Lucy and Zoey would calm down, and he asked me how school had been.

Up until then, I hadn't realized I was still upset about Michelle, but I suddenly burst into tears. Everybody stopped eating and looked at me. Even Lucy and Zoey stopped fussing. I don't cry very often, so everybody was startled.

"Wow," Dad said. "What happened at school?"

Papa handed me a tissue. I blew my nose and told them about the field trip and about Michelle.

"I'm going to go on that field trip if I have to drag myself up all those stairs with my fingernails," I said.

Dad laughed. "I'm pretty sure we'll figure out a better arrangement than that."

"Have you ever been to Fort Symons?" Papa asked Dad. "It's really not handicapped accessible. It has that tower, too. I wish Mr. Nguyen had talked to us before he announced the trip."

"I'm still going," I said to Papa. "I'm pretty sure I could forge your signature on the permission slip."

He gave me a look. "I'll call Mr. Nguyen after supper," he said. "We'll try to work something out."

After supper, I started working on my homework while Papa called Mr. Nguyen. It was hard to pay attention to math problems when I was trying to hear what Papa was saying. I could hear his voice but not most of the words, since he'd gone down the hall into his study. Finally, I gave up on homework and rolled down the hall to eavesdrop.

"Yes," I heard Papa say, and then, "Well, no, no, of course not." There was a pause and then Papa said, "That sounds good. Let me know what works best for everyone."

Papa looked up then and saw me sitting in the doorway. He frowned at me, because he knew I'd

been trying to eavesdrop, but he motioned for me to come in the rest of the way. "Okay, then," he said into the phone, "we'll be in touch."

He hung up and his frown turned into a smile. "We'll work something out," he said. "It will be okay. We're going to meet with Mr. Nguyen and some other people from your school next week and decide what the best solution would be."

"Can I come to the meeting?" I asked.

"Absolutely," he said. "It's your trip; you should be part of this decision."

I tried not to think about the field trip. I went to a movie on Friday night with Mia and Rachel, and that got my mind off things for a while. I love how movies let you live someone else's life for a couple of hours. I also like to get ideas for my own movies, like thinking about the different camera angles the director used and stuff like that.

The meeting was set for the next Thursday evening. I was nervous about it. At school on Thursday, I kept having trouble focusing. I was afraid the people at the meeting were going to say, "That's too bad, Sierra. Maybe we can find someone to watch you at school while everyone else is out having fun. We can get you to do extra math problems or something."

Well, okay, I didn't really think they'd make me do extra math. At least, I hoped they wouldn't.

I was so distracted in gym class that I didn't catch the basketball at all when people threw it to me. I'm not usually that bad in gym. Just because I'm in a wheelchair, doesn't mean I can't catch a ball. Well, usually it doesn't. I threw the ball at the basket and didn't even come close. In fact, I came a lot closer to hitting my gym teacher in the head. I was glad the meeting would be over with by tonight.

At five minutes before seven that evening, I was at the school with Dad and Papa. Auntie Nina, Dad's sister, had come over to the house to watch Lucy and Zoey.

The meeting was in my classroom. Mr. Nguyen was there, along with the principal, the special ed teacher, and some other people I didn't know. One of these people, a woman named Kate Engelbright, turned out to be a representative from Fort Symons.

After I realized they weren't really trying to make me stay at school while everyone else went on the field trip, I relaxed a little. The choice seemed to be between going to a different site for the field trip— one that *was* handicapped accessible—or else figuring out some way to make Fort Symons work for me. The problem with the first option was that there really weren't any other good Revolutionary War sites nearby.

So, in order for me to go on the field trip, I had to either agree not to worry about going upstairs in the fort or someone would have to carry me up the stairs.

I didn't want to just stay downstairs. I didn't want to be left behind while everyone else got to see every-thing. Everybody was worried, though, about the liability of having someone carry me up the stairs, in case they dropped me.

"This is ridiculous," Dad finally said. "I'll go along and carry Sierra."

Eventually, everybody agreed that it would be okay if Dad went on the field trip and carried me up the stairs at Fort Symons. Dad and Papa signed some-thing that said they were responsible for me. I was really glad Dad was going to be the one to carry me. I hadn't liked the idea of somebody I didn't know very well doing it. It's a personal thing, being carried. I felt lucky I had a Dad who *could* carry me.

"Do you mind doing this?" I asked Dad on the way home from the meeting.

"No, of course not," he said. "It's a field trip for me, too. I'm going to take the day off work, after all."

After a minute, I asked Dad and Papa, "Do you ever feel cheated that you adopted a broken kid?"

"No!" said Dad, and Papa said, "You, Sierra, are far from broken."

"When you adopted Zoey and Lucy, was it because you wanted to have some healthy kids for a change?" I couldn't quite let it go.

"We adopted Zoey and Lucy because we wanted more kids," Papa said. "We love you exactly the way you are."

"We've never regretted adopting you," Dad said. "Never, ever."

A month later, on the day of the field trip, I was so excited I could hardly eat breakfast, but Dad made me eat anyway.

Dad and I rode on the bus with the rest of the class, which was an extra bonus. I didn't usually get to ride the bus. I sat with Mia, and Rachel sat in front of us. I had brought my video camera, of course, so I could film the whole trip.

Once we got to Fort Symons, everybody stampeded off the bus, but Mia and Rachel stayed back to wait for me. Dad got my wheelchair, took it off the bus, and unfolded it, then came back to get me.

Once I got settled in the chair, Dad pushed it so I could have my hands free to film. I got a great shot of the fort rising up against the blue, blue sky. It was a perfect day for filming.

The inside of the fort was great, all dim and interesting. I thought it would make a great set for a film, although I'd need to bring in more light if I wanted to do that.

Then it was time to go upstairs. Most people were already up there. I could hear them running around and calling to each other.

"Ready?" Dad asked, and I nodded.

He picked me up and I wrapped one arm around his neck, leaving the other one free to hold my camera. Mr. Nguyen picked up the wheelchair and carried it up the stairs behind us.

"Let's do the tower first," I said, so he headed toward a dark opening in the corner.

The stairs up to the top of the tower were dark and spooky, and I was pretty sure my camera wasn't going to pick up much in there, but I felt totally safe in my dad's arms.

Suddenly, the darkness got less and then we broke out into the brilliant sunlight.

"Oh, wow!" I said. I could see the land spread out all around the fort. Our bus down in the parking lot was tiny, like a toy.

Mr. Nguyen hadn't carried my wheelchair up the tower stairs, so Dad kept holding me.

"Are you getting tired?" I asked him.

"I'm fine," he said. "This is an amazing view, isn't it?"

"Maybe I could come back and film a Rapunzel story here." I paused. "Dad, I'm not always going to have someone to carry me. I guess I won't always get to see the top of towers. So, thanks. Thanks for doing this."

"You're welcome," he said. "But you were the one who was determined enough to make this happen.

You'll always find a way to get what you want out of life, and you won't let the wheelchair stop you. I know you."

I smiled and put my head on his shoulder. Because he was right. I would always want to see the tops of towers—and I wasn't about to let anything stop me.

Kids and Physical Challenges

Almost one in five people in the United States has some sort of *physical disability*, and as many as one in eight children is physically *challenged* in some way. Kids with physical challenges have trouble seeing, hearing, walking, speaking, lifting, or doing other activities. Many kids have what is called a *severe* physical disability, and cannot do one or more of these things without using a wheelchair or some other type of help.

A physical disability can make many things more difficult, but it's only part of who a person is. Though they may do things differently, kids with physical challenges are not very different from other kids. They can be just as smart, friendly, and successful in school as other children. Always remember that kids with physical challenges deserve the same respect that all kids do.

Physical has to do with your body.

A disability is a condition that makes it harder for a person to do the things that other people do.

If you are challenged, that means you are faced with something hard to handle.

Severe means very serious or bad.

A child with a physical disability may not be able to walk the way other kids do. Some children with physical challenges cannot walk at all and must use a wheelchair to get from place to place. A physical challenge affects a kid's ability to do everyday activities in some way.

Physical challenges come in many different forms. Each disability is different. Many kids with physical challenges are able to succeed at school and do daily activities with some help.

A child with a severe physical disability may need a wheelchair to move around.

What Causes Physical Challenges?

Some children are born with physical challenges. These types of disability can be caused by injuries that babies can get while being born or before birth. If there is a problem with the way the baby forms in the mother's *womb*, the baby may be born with a physical disability. Some problems can lead to a baby's arm or leg forming incorrectly, for instance. Certain physical disabilities may be easily seen when a baby is born, while others may not. Cerebral palsy, a disorder that cannot be immediately seen because it affects a child's *nervous system*, causes physical disability. So does spina bifida.

The *womb* is the part of a woman's body where a baby grows during pregnancy.

The *nervous system* is made up of your brain, your spinal cord, and the enormous network of nerves that runs throughout your body. Your brain uses information it receives from your nerves to coordinate all of your actions and reactions.

If a child is not born with a physical challenge, he can become physically challenged later in life in the following ways:

- *Injuries and accidents*: Kids can become physically challenged after of an injury or bad accident. A fall,

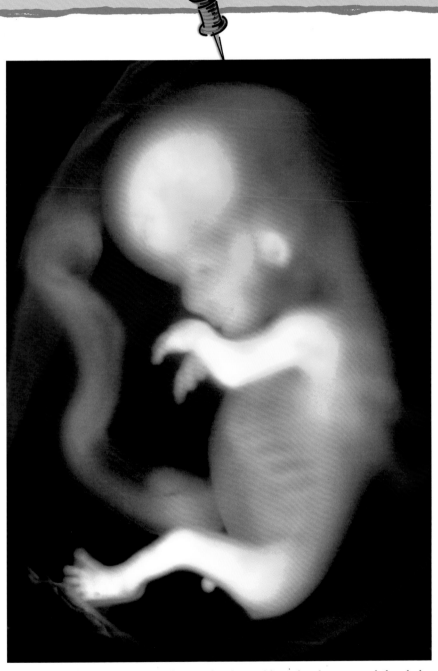

Some physical disabilities are the result of a problem that happens while a baby is still in its mother's womb.

sports injury, fire, or other accident can lead to a physical disability.

- *Disease and illness*: Certain diseases and conditions can cause physical disability. Here are a few other conditions or diseases that can lead to physical disabilities:
  - muscular dystrophy
  - multiple sclerosis
  - *diabetes*
  - some heart and lung problems
  - some head injuries
  - spine injuries

Types of Physical Challenges

The term "physical challenges" covers many different types of disabilities, including:

- *amputation*: In some cases when a person is injured or sick, doctors may need to remove an arm or leg. Often the limb is removed to keep an injury or illness from doing more damage to a person's body. This is

Diabetes (sometimes called "sugar diabetes") is a disease that gets in the way of the body using glucose (a type of sugar) the way it should. Glucose is the main source of energy for the body's cells, and its levels in the blood are controlled by a chemical called insulin, which helps the glucose get to the cells where it's needed. In diabetes, the pancreas does not make enough insulin or the body can't respond normally to the insulin that is made. This makes glucose levels in the blood rise, which in turn can cause other health problems.

Diabetes is a disease that can cause physical disabilities if it is not kept under control. This father is helping his daughter test her blood sugar level as part of her diabetes care.

called amputation. People who have had a limb removed are called amputees. Amputees may have their removed limb replaced with a *prosthetic* arm, hand, or leg.

- *limb differences*: A person with a limb difference is born with a limb that is not fully formed, is shaped differently from other people's limbs, or is missing altogether.

Prosthetic means that something is an artificial replacement, such as an arm or leg that is made from plastic and metal to replace a normal arm or leg.

- *cerebral palsy (CP)*: This condition is caused by damage to the brain before, during, or just after birth. Kids with cerebral palsy have trouble moving because of damage to the part of the brain that controls movement. CP can result in the loss of movement in the legs, one side of the body, both arms and legs, or the entire body. Many kids with CP use crutches, a wheelchair, or other forms of help to get around. Cerebral palsy has no cure.

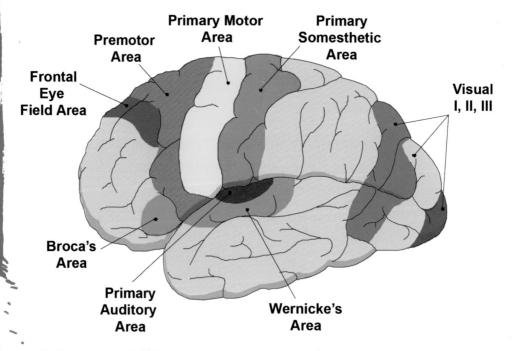

Different areas of the brain control different parts of the body. Damage to certain areas can lead to physical challenges.

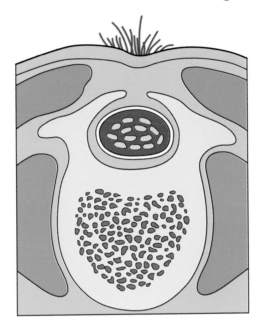

This is an illustration of spina bifida. The top image shows a normal bone in the spine, with the spinal cord enclosed by bone.

The lower image shows the spinal cord bulging out because the bone did not form around the cord as it should have.

- *spinal cord injury (SCI)*: An injury to the spinal cord can cause serious physical disability. The type of physical difficulties that a person will have after a spinal cord injury depends on where the spine is damaged. A person may not be able to walk after an injury to the lower part of his spine, for example. If an injury is higher up on the spine, the injured person may not be able to move both his legs and his

Four-year-old Erin Burney has muscular dystrophy, a disorder that causes all her muscles to weaken.

arms. An injury near the neck can cause a person to lose use of her muscles from the neck down. People with SCI often need to use a wheelchair or other help to move.

- *spina bifida*: *Spina* means "spine" and bifida means "in two." This means that the spinal column has not formed around the spinal cord the way it is supposed to. There are a few types of spina bifida, the most common caused by the spinal cord sticking through the spinal column. Spina bifida causes many of the same effects of SCI, including loss of muscle movement.
- *muscular dystrophy (MD)*: Muscular dystrophy is the name for a few different disorders that all cause muscles to weaken over time. Muscular dystrophy is genetic and has no cure. Different types of MD affect children and adults. One of the most common types of MD, Duchenne dystrophy (DMD), affects only boys. Almost all boys born with DMD will need to use a wheelchair by the time they are teenagers.

Physical Challenges and Treatment

Many kids with physical challenges will need help learning to do everyday activities. Kids with physical challenges may also need to see certain doctors who are experts in their kind of disability. Here are a few of the people that kids with physical challenges may need to see:

- *Orthopedists*: doctors who are experts on bones and muscles.
- *Neurologists*: doctors who are experts on disorders that affect the nervous system.
- *Physical **therapists***: ***specialists*** who help kids learn to use their biggest muscles to move. This might mean help with walking, standing, using a wheelchair or crutches, sitting, or other daily activities.
- *Occupational therapists*: specialists who work with smaller muscles and smaller movements. Occupational therapists help kids with things like hand and finger movements used in everyday activities (using a pencil, for example, or brushing their teeth).

> ***Therapists*** *are people who are skilled in a special kind of treatment for a disease or condition.*
>
> ***Specialists*** *are people who focus on a particular medical area and are experts in that area.*

- *Speech/language therapists*: specialists who help kids improve speaking and language understanding. Kids who have a physical disability that affects their ability to speak or hear might see a speech/language therapist.
- *Ophthalmologists*: doctors who are experts on eyes and eye disorders.

- *Prosthetists*: specialists who design and fit prosthetic limbs. Prothetists also work with kids who need braces to support their muscles.

Having a physical disability does not mean a child needs to be inactive.

Kids with Physical Challenges and Assistive Technology Devices

Assistive technology *devices* (ATDs) help many kids with physical challenges. These devices make certain tasks easier for kids who are physically challenged. Here are a few examples of ATDs:

- Many children with physical disabilities use a wheelchair. Wheelchairs come in many different forms, including wheelchairs built for sports like basketball, racing, and tennis.

> *Assistive means helpful.*
>
> *Devices are instruments invented to serve a special purpose.*

- Many kids with physical challenges also use crutches to help them stand, balance, and walk.
- Electric elevators help children who use wheelchairs get upstairs, and in and out of cars or buses.
- Braces help children whose muscles need support.
- Kids who can't use both hands might have special computers that are activated by their voices.
- Prosthetic limbs can help people who are missing a limb to walk, run, pick things up, and do other daily activities.

Physical Challenges and School

Many kids with physical challenges are excellent students. With changes in the classroom and the right help, kids with physical disabilities can learn and do well in school.

Since so many children with physical disabilities need to use some sort of ATD to move around, it's important

Schools and other buildings need to have ramps and elevators so that kids in wheelchairs or other ATDs are able to get in and move around the building easily.

that the school is *accessible* to kids with physical challenges. The school may need to have a ramp for wheelchairs or an elevator to get to higher floors. In the United States, a law called the ***Rehabilitation*** Act of 1973 requires that

Accessible *means that something can be easily reached.*

Rehabilitation *is the process of helping someone get back to normal after an illness or injury.*

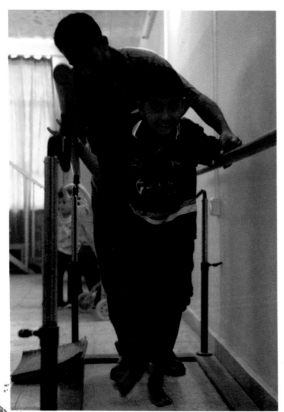

Physical therapy can help a child with a physical disability learn to use his muscles better.

schools getting money from the government make buildings accessible to kids with physical disabilities.

Kids with physical challenges may also do better with some changes in the classroom. These changes are often small ones, such as making sure that the classroom has wide, uncluttered aisles, so that a student using crutches, braces, or a wheelchair can move around more easily.

Kids with Physical Challenges and Special Education

For many children with physical challenges, *special education* will be the best way for them to succeed in school. Through special education, kids with physical disabilities can get help from physical, occupational, and speech-language therapists.

Special education teaches kids who have trouble learning because of some disability.

To qualify means to fit the definition of something or to meet the requirements.

A law called the Individuals with Disabilities Education Act (IDEA) outlines how schools should decide which kids need special education. In order to *qualify* for special education under IDEA, the child's physical challenge must get in the way of his learn-

41

A child with a physical disability might do things a little differently than you, but he can still be a fun person and great friend!

ing new material, understanding schoolwork, or taking part in school activities.

The IDEA law lists thirteen different kinds of disabilities that may mean a child will qualify for special education. Physical challenges and disabilities are covered in the "*orthopedic impairment*" *category* under the law.

The IDEA law requires that:

- the child has problems performing well at school activities.
- the child's parent, teacher, or other school staff person must ask that the child be examined for a disability.
- the child is *evaluated* to decide if she does indeed have a disability and to figure out what kind of special education she needs.
- a group of people, including the kid's parents, teachers, and an expert on the kid's physical disability, meets to decide on a plan for helping him. This plan is called an Individualized Education Program (IEP). The IEP spells out exactly what the child needs in order to succeed at school.

Orthopedic has to do with the medical treatment of the skeleton.

An impairment is something that damages a person's abilities in some way.

A category is a group or a certain kind of thing.

When something is evaluated, it is examined to see in which category it belongs.

Succeeding with Physical Challenges

When you see a kid with a physical challenge, the first thing you notice may be her crutches or her wheelchair. But a child with a physical challenge is much more than her disability.

Physical challenges don't stop a kid from being friendly or funny or smart. He may still be good at sports (even if he has to play games a little differently from other kids). Kids with physical challenges may do other things differently than you do, but that doesn't mean they are strange or weird. In most ways, they are kids just like you. You can make their life easier by treating them with respect— and by getting to know them.

Further Reading

Abramovitz, M. *Muscular Dystrophy*. San Diego, Calif.: Lucent Books, 2008.

Bjorklund, R. *Cerebral Palsy*. New York: Benchmark Books, 2006.

Brill, M. T. *Multiple Sclerosis*. New York: Benchmark Books, 2007.

Johnson, P. *Muscular Dystrophy*. New York: Rosen Publishing, 2008.

Kent, D. *Athletes With Disabilities*. London, UK: Franklin Watts, 2003.

Landau, E. *Spinal Cord Injuries*. Berkeley Heights, N.J.: Enslow Publishers, 2001.

Levete, S. *Explaining Cerebral Palsy*. North Mankato, Minn.: Smart Apple Media, 2009.

Parker, Steve. *Spinal Cord and Nerves*. Mankato, Minn.: Heinemann Library, 2003.

Watson, S. *Spina Bifida*. New York: Rosen Publishing, 2008.

Find Out More On the Internet

Ability OnLine
www.ablelink.org

Amputee Coalition of America
www.amputee-coalition.org

Canadian Paralympic Committee (CPC)
www.paralympic.ca

Muscular Dystrophy Association (MDA)
www.mda.org

The National Center on Physical Activity and Disability (NCPAD)
www.ncpad.org

National Dissemination Center for Children with Disabilities (NICHY)
www.nichy.org

The National Spinal Cord Injury Association
www.spinalcord.org

National Sports Center for the Disabled
www.nscd.org

Spina Bifida Association of America
www.sbaa.org

United Cerebral Palsy (UCP)
www.ucp.org

Disclaimer

The websites listed on this page were active at the time of publication. The publisher is not responsible for websites that have changed their address or discontinued operation since the date of publication. The publisher will review and update the websites upon each reprint.

Index

About the Authors

Sheila Stewart has written several dozen books for young people, both fiction and nonfiction, although she especially enjoys writing fiction. She has a master's degree in English and now works as a writer and editor. She lives with her two children in a house overflowing with books, in the Southern Tier of New York State.

Camden Flath is a writer living and working in Binghamton, New York. He has a degree in English and has written several books for young people. He is interested in current political, social, and economic issues and applies those interests to his writing.

About the Consultant

Dr. Carolyn Bridgemohan is board certified in developmental behavioral pediatrics and practices at the Developmental Medicine Center at Children's Hospital Boston. She is the director of the Autism Care Program and an assistant professor at Harvard Medical School. Her specialty areas are autism and other pervasive developmental disorders, developmental and learning problems, and developmental and behavioral pediatrics.